Primo dizionario illustrato
Animali

First Picture Dictionary
Animals

Maiale
Pig

Coniglio
Rabbit

Farfalla
Butterfly

Volpe
Fox

Illustrato da Anna Ivanir

www.kidkiddos.com
Copyright ©2025 by KidKiddos Books Ltd.
support@kidkiddos.com

All rights reserved. No part of this book may be reproduced in any form or by any electronic or mechanical means, including information storage and retrieval systems, without written permission from the publisher, except in the case of a reviewer, who may quote brief passages embodied in critical articles or in a review.
First edition, 2025

Library and Archives Canada Cataloguing in Publication
First Picture Dictionary – Animals (Italian English Bilingual edition)
ISBN: 978-1-83416-291-1 paperback
ISBN: 978-1-83416-292-8 hardcover
ISBN: 978-1-83416-290-4 eBook

Animali selvatici
Wild Animals

Leone
Lion

Tigre
Tiger

Giraffa
Giraffe

✦ *La giraffa è l'animale terrestre più alto.*
✦ A giraffe is the tallest animal on land.

Elefante
Elephant

Scimmia
Monkey

Animali selvatici
Wild Animals

Ippopotamo
Hippopotamus

Panda
Panda

Volpe
Fox

Rinoceronte
Rhino

Cervo
Deer

Alce
Moose

Lupo
Wolf

✦ *L'alce è un ottimo nuotatore e può immergersi per mangiare piante!*
✦ A moose is a great swimmer and can dive underwater to eat plants!

Scoiattolo
Squirrel

Koala
Koala

✦ *Lo scoiattolo nasconde le noci per l'inverno, ma a volte dimentica dove le ha messe!*
✦ A squirrel hides nuts for winter, but sometimes forgets where it put them!

Gorilla
Gorilla

Animali domestici
Pets

Canarino
Canary

Porcellino d'India
Guinea Pig

✦ *La rana può respirare sia attraverso la pelle che con i polmoni!*

✦ A frog can breathe through its skin as well as its lungs!

Rana
Frog

Criceto
Hamster

Pesce rosso
Goldfish

Cane
Dog

✦ *Alcuni pappagalli possono imitare le parole e perfino ridere come un essere umano!*

✦ *Some parrots can copy words and even laugh like a human!*

Gatto
Cat

Pappagallo
Parrot

Animali della fattoria
Animals at the Farm

Mucca
Cow

Gallina
Chicken

Anatra
Duck

Pecora
Sheep

Cavallo
Horse

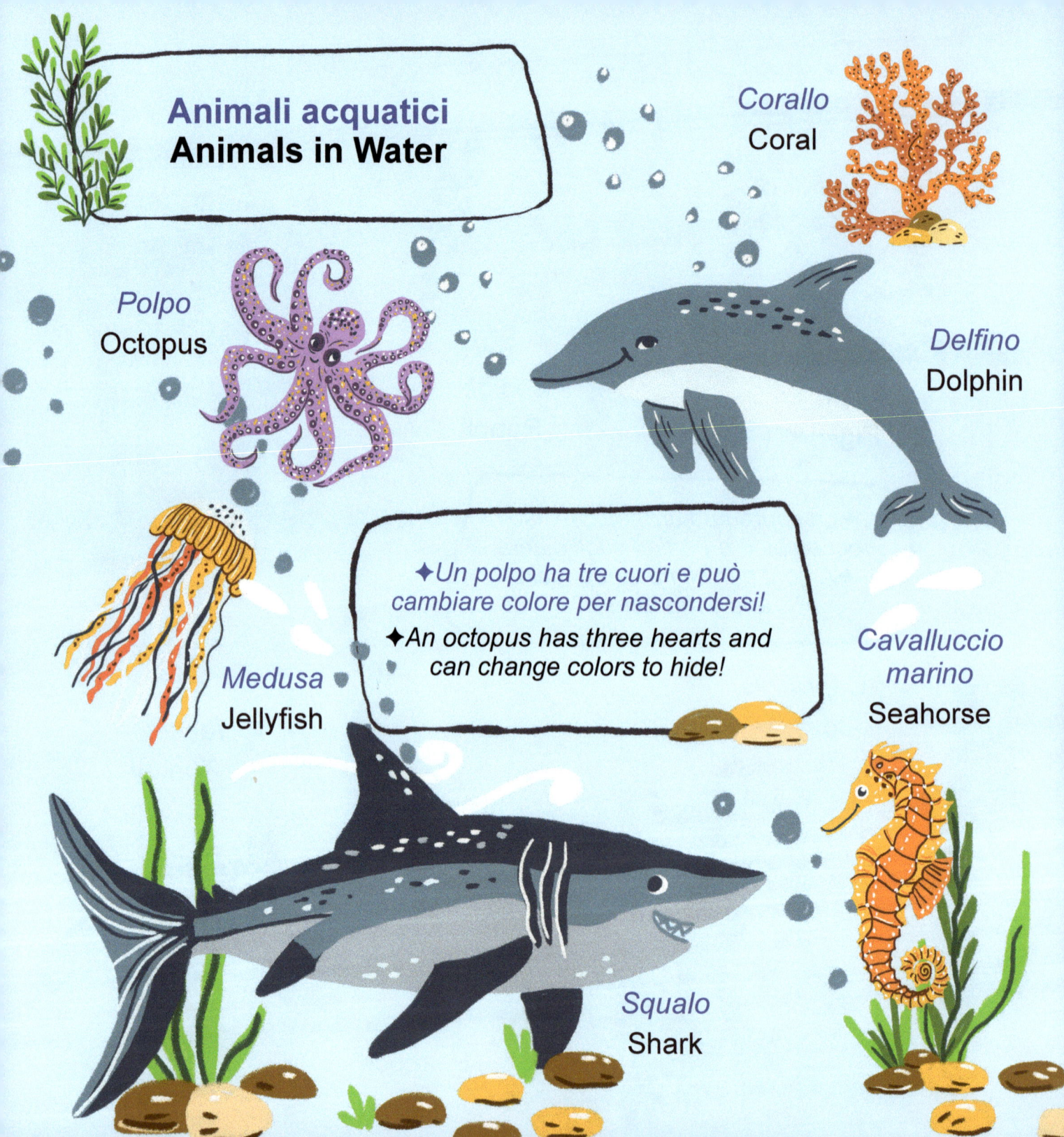

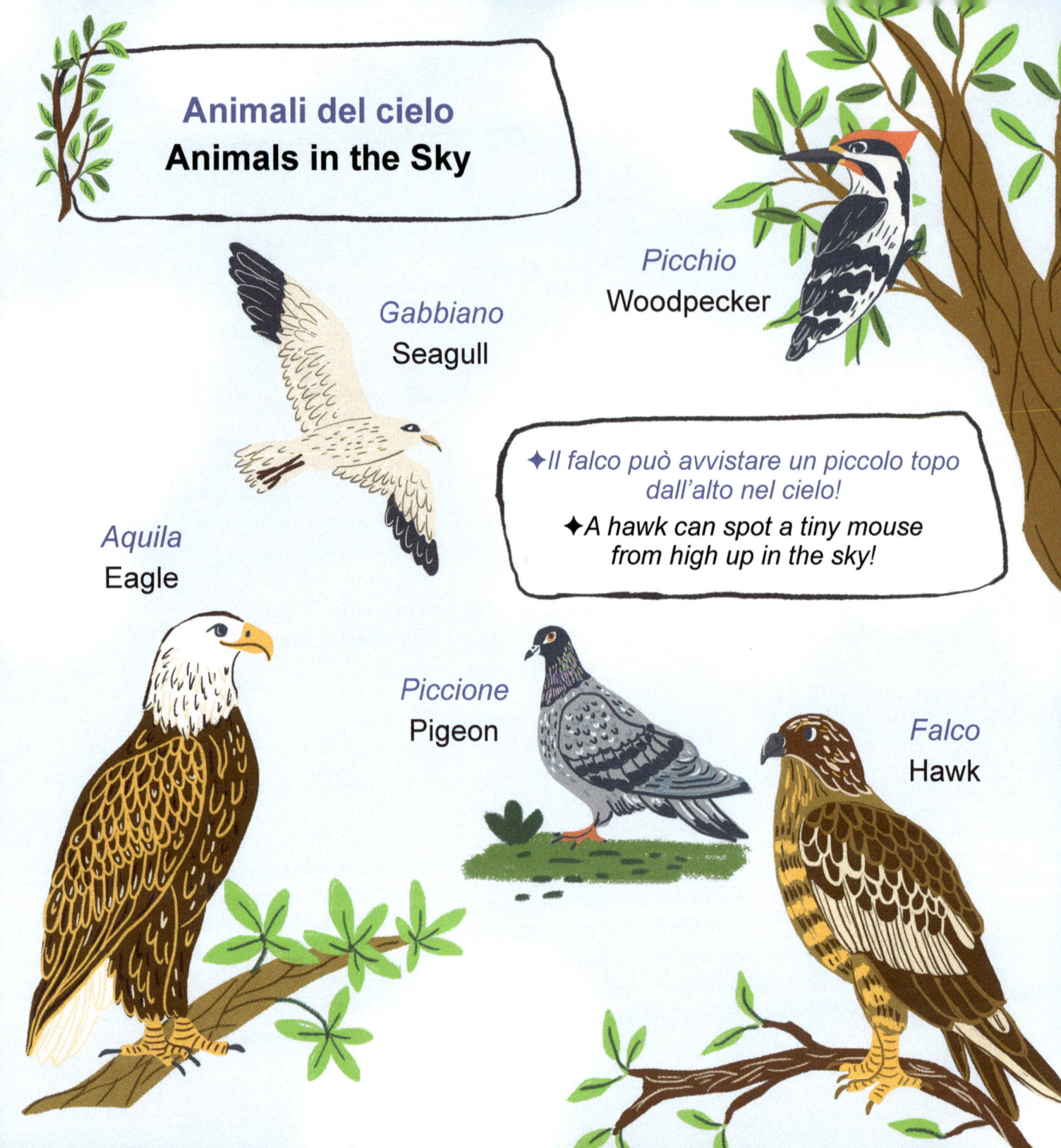

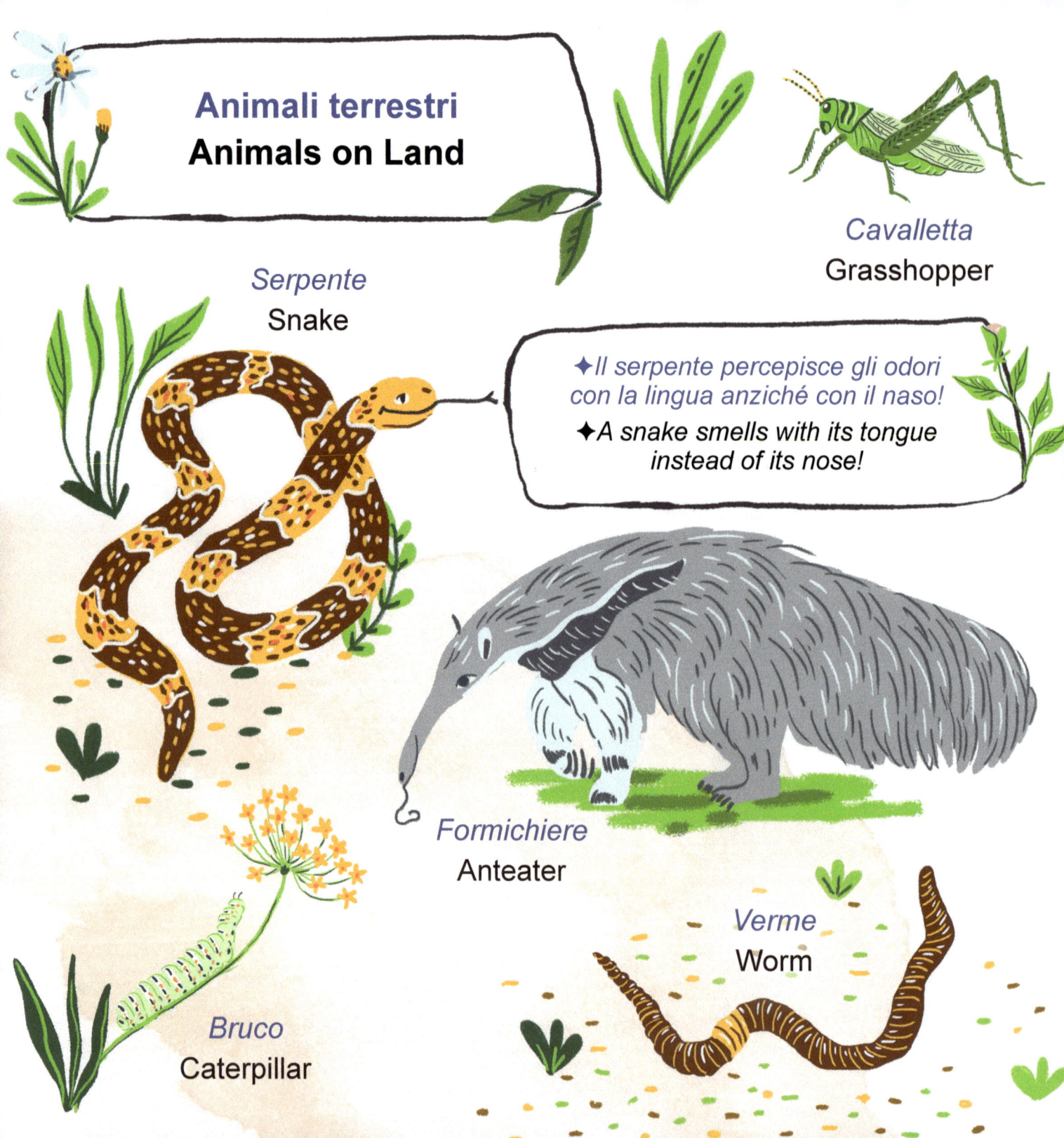

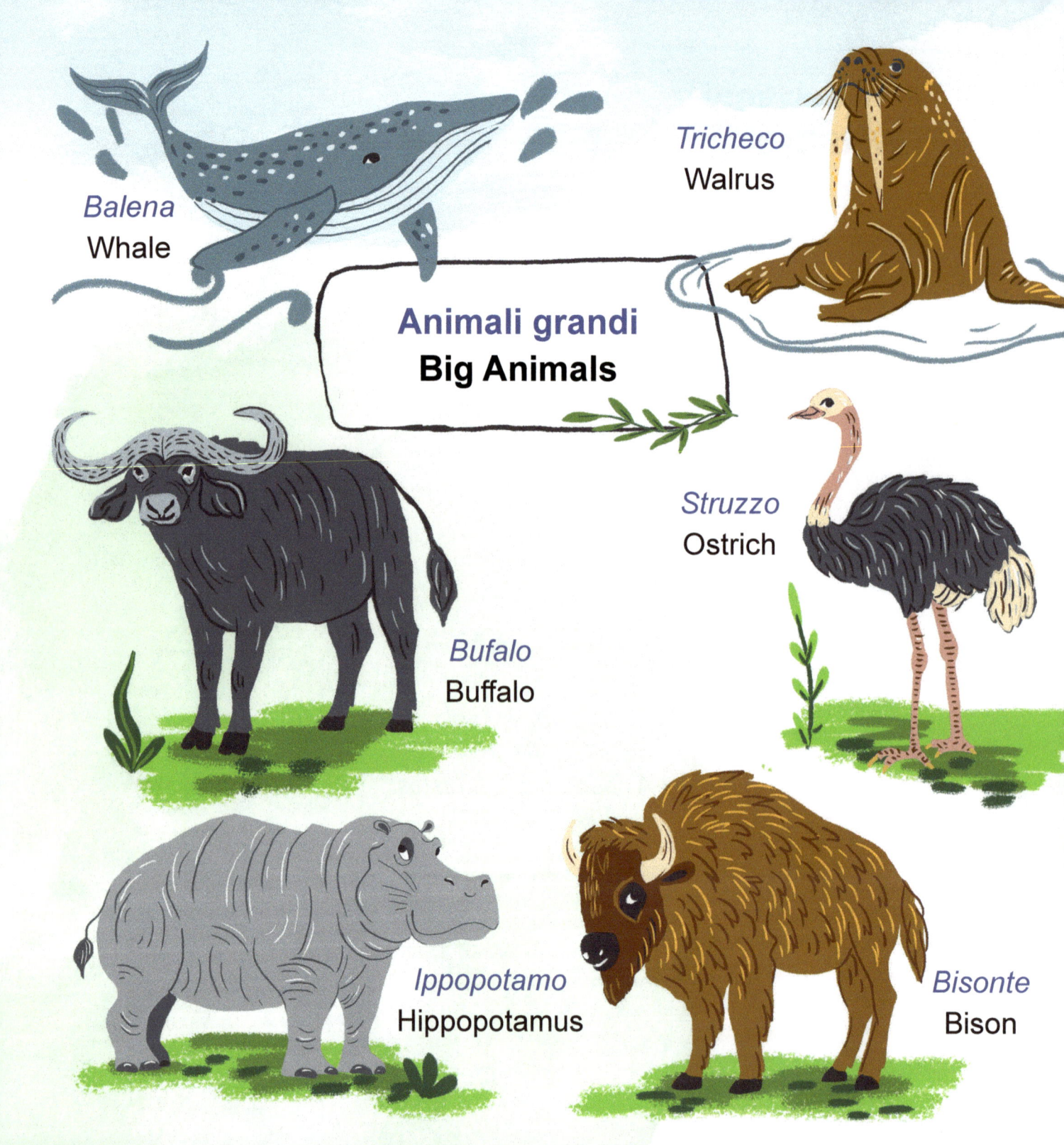

Animali piccoli
Small Animals

Camaleonte
Chameleon

Ragno
Spider

✦ *Lo struzzo è l'uccello più grande, ma non può volare!*
✦ An ostrich is the biggest bird, but it cannot fly!

Ape
Bee

✦ *La lumaca porta la sua casa sulla schiena e si muove molto lentamente.*
✦ A snail carries its home on its back and moves very slowly.

Lumaca
Snail

Topo
Mouse

Animali silenziosi
Quiet Animals

Tartaruga
Turtle

Coccinella
Ladybug

✦ *La tartaruga può vivere sia sulla terra che in acqua.*
✦ A turtle can live both on land and in water.

Pesce
Fish

Lucertola
Lizard

Gufo
Owl

Pipistrello
Bat

✦ *Il gufo caccia di notte e usa il suo udito per trovare il cibo!*
✦ An owl hunts at night and uses its hearing to find food!

✦ *La lucciola si illumina di notte per trovare altre lucciole.*
✦ A firefly glows at night to find other fireflies.

Procione
Raccoon

Tarantola
Tarantula

Animali colorati
Colorful Animals

Il fenicottero è rosa
A flamingo is pink

Il gufo è marrone
An owl is brown

Il cigno è bianco
A swan is white

Il polpo è viola
An octopus is purple

La rana è verde
A frog is green

✦ *La rana è verde, così può nascondersi tra le foglie.*
✦ A frog is green, so it can hide among the leaves.

L'orso polare è bianco
A polar bear is white

La volpe è arancione
A fox is orange

Il koala è grigio
A koala is grey

La pantera è nera
A panther is black

Il pulcino è giallo
A chick is yellow

Animali e i loro piccoli
Animals and Their Babies

Mucca e Vitello
Cow and Calf

Gatto e Gattino
Cat and Kitten

Gallina e Pulcino
Chicken and Chick

✦ *Il pulcino parla con sua madre ancora prima di nascere*
✦ A chick talks to its mother even before it hatches.

Cane e Cucciolo
Dog and Puppy

www.ingramcontent.com/pod-product-compliance
Lightning Source LLC
LaVergne TN
LVHW071118080526
838200LV00079B/4784